5 ESSENTIALS FOR LIFELONG INTIMACY

DR. JAMES DOBSON

Multnomah® Publishers *Sisters, Oregon*

5 ESSENTIALS FOR LIFELONG INTIMACY
published by Multnomah Publishers, Inc.

© 2005 by James Dobson, Inc.
International Standard Book Number: 1-59052-377-6

Cover image in lower right corner by Ellen Denuto/Getty Images
Interior typeset by Katherine Lloyd, The DESK

Unless otherwise indicated, Scripture quotations are from:
The Holy Bible, New International Version
© 1973, 1984 by International Bible Society,
used by permission of Zondervan Publishing House

Other Scripture quotations are from:
The Holy Bible, King James Version (KJV).
The Living Bible (TLB) © 1971. Used by permission of
Tyndale House Publishers, Inc. All rights reserved.

Multnomah is a trademark of Multnomah Publishers, Inc.,
and is registered in the U.S. Patent and Trademark Office.
The colophon is a trademark of Multnomah Publishers, Inc.

Printed in the United States of America

For information:
MULTNOMAH PUBLISHERS, INC.
POST OFFICE BOX 1720
SISTERS, OREGON 97759

05 06 07 08 09 10—10 9 8 7 6 5 4 3 2 1 0

Contents

Acknowledgments

I want to thank my editor, Jim Lund, for his assistance in helping to research, compile, and shape the material in this book. Once again, it has been a pleasure to work with him.

Appreciation is also expressed to everyone on the team at Multnomah for their efforts in bringing this book to life.

Introduction

Nanette and Paul began their marriage with the highest of hopes. They both enjoyed the outdoors, especially horseback riding, and loved to travel. Paul already had a successful brokerage business, so they could afford a beautiful lakefront home. Both wanted children. Best of all, they relished every minute they were together. They were soul mates, deeply in love. It seemed nothing could go wrong.

As the years passed, however, *everything* began to unravel. Though Nanette and Paul were thrilled by the birth of two daughters, the demands of parenting placed an unexpected strain on their relationship. Then Paul's business began to fail, and he found himself spending more and more hours at the office. To help keep up with payments on the house and a new boat, as well as the increasing costs of raising kids, Nanette took a job as a dental assistant. She and Paul saw less and less of each other, and when they did, they argued often.

It was a rainy night in November, during a particularly heated fight, when Nanette's worst fears were confirmed: Paul was seeing another woman. As the tears ran down her face, Nanette remembered the closeness she and Paul once shared. She wondered, *How did our marriage ever come to this?* Their once-idyllic relationship had been ripped to shreds. The divorce was finalized less than a year later.

The story of Nanette and Paul is a common one. For every ten marriages in America today, five will end in bitter conflict and divorce. That is tragic, but have you ever wondered what happens to the other five? Do they sail blissfully into the sunset? Hardly!

According to clinical psychologist Neil Warren, all five of these "successful" marriages will stay together for a lifetime, but in varying degrees of disharmony. On a *Focus on the Family* radio broadcast, Dr. Warren quoted the research of Dr. John Cuber, whose findings were published in a book entitled *The Significant Americans*. Cuber learned that some couples will remain married for the benefit of the children, while others will pass the years in relative apathy. Incredibly, only one or two couples in ten will achieve what might be called "intimacy" in their marriages.

By *intimacy*, Dr. Cuber was referring to the mystical bond of friendship, understanding, and commitment that almost defies explanation. It occurs when a man and woman, starting out as separate and distinct individuals, fuse into a single unit, which the Bible calls "one flesh." I'm convinced that the human spirit craves this kind of unconditional love and that women, especially, experience something akin to "soul hunger" when it cannot be achieved. I'm also certain that most couples expect to find intimacy in marriage, yet somehow it often eludes them.

Despite their desire for a soul-deep closeness, many couples today—including those who are already wed—also *fear* intimacy. They have watched friends and perhaps their own parents tear their marriages and each other to pieces. Now these men and women are afraid of being vulnerable—of being rejected and abandoned. Some wonder if true intimacy with another human being is even achievable in our modern world.

Fortunately, marital partners are not merely passive victims in the unfolding drama of their lives together. They *can* build a stable, satisfying, intimate relationship that will withstand the storms of life. Neither divorce nor a lifeless marriage is inevitable. After the blessing of more than forty years of marriage to my wife, Shirley, I can say that there is nothing quite like being loved intimately and unconditionally, decade after decade, by someone who promises to be there for better or worse, in sickness and health, whether richer or poorer, forsaking all others—*all* others—until separated by death. A soul-to-soul relationship under the umbrella of marriage is a plan that bears the wisdom and compassion of the Creator Himself, and it offers the greatest satisfaction in human experience.

There are many tools that can help you lovingly bond to your mate, but at least five components are *essential* to enjoying a close relationship for a lifetime. As we explore them together, including the tips that follow each chapter, I pray that they will give you fresh inspiration for renewing and deepening intimacy in your marriage.

A Christ-Centered Home

*No one can lay any foundation other than the one
already laid, which is Jesus Christ.*

1 CORINTHIANS 3:11

S ome years ago, in an effort to draw on the
experiences of those who have lived together
harmoniously as husbands and wives, we
asked married couples to participate in an informal
study. More than six hundred people agreed to
speak candidly about the concepts and methods
that have succeeded in their homes for thirty, forty,
or even fifty years. They each wrote comments and

recommendations, which were carefully analyzed and compared. The advice they offered is not new, but it certainly represents a great place to begin. In attempting to learn any task, one should begin with the fundamentals—those initial steps from which everything else will develop.

What, then, according to our seasoned panel of experts, is the single most important key to enjoying a successful marriage—the *one* thing most likely to guarantee a lifetime of intimacy and love?

The answer is to establish and maintain a Christ-centered home.

When a husband and wife are deeply committed to Jesus Christ, they enjoy enormous advantages over a family with no spiritual dimension. Everything rests on that foundation. Only through a spiritual connection to Him can we experience genuine love and begin to fulfill all the potential of the relationship we call marriage.

I once received the following letter:

Dear Dr. Dobson:

My husband recently left me after fifteen years of marriage. We had a great physical, emotional, and intellectual relationship. But something was missing...we had no spiritual bond between us.

Please tell young couples that there will always be a void in their lives together without Christ. A good marriage must have its foundation in Him in order to experience lasting love, peace, and joy.

Since my husband walked out on me, I have tried to rebuild my relationship with God. I am now growing steadily in my walk with the Lord, but I am alone.

There is great truth in this sad letter. Our Lord, after all, *created* marriage, one of the most marvelous and enduring gifts ever bestowed on humankind.

This divine plan was revealed to Adam and Eve in the Garden of Eden and then described succinctly in Genesis 2:24, where we read, "Therefore shall a man leave his father and his mother, and shall cleave unto his wife: and they shall be one flesh" (KJV). With those twenty-one words, God announced the ordination of the family. Five thousand years of recorded history have come and gone, yet every civilization in the history of the world has been built upon it. To expect a loving, intimate marriage without relying on the Lord is foolhardy indeed.

To expect a loving, intimate marriage without relying on the Lord is foolhardy.

In contrast, the couple that depends on Scripture for solutions to the stresses of living has a distinct advantage over the family with no faith. The Bible they love is the world's most wonderful text. It was written by thirty-nine authors who spoke three separate languages and lived in a time frame spanning fifteen hundred years. How miraculous is the work of those inspired writers! If two or three individuals today were to witness a bank robbery, they would probably give conflicting accounts of the incident. Human perception is simply that flawed. Yet those thirty-nine contributors to Scripture, most of whom never even met each other, prepared sixty-six separate books that fit together with perfect continuity and symmetry. The entire Old Testament makes a single statement: "Jesus is coming." And the New Testament declares: "Jesus is here!"

By reading these Holy Scriptures, we are given a window into the mind of the Father. What an infallible resource! The Creator, who began with nothingness and made beautiful mountains and streams and clouds and cuddly little babies, has elected to give us the inside story of the family. He tells us in His Word how to live together in peace and harmony. Everything from handling money to sexual attitudes is discussed in Scripture, with each prescription bearing the personal endorsement of the King of the universe. Why would anyone disregard the truths revealed therein?

The Christian way of life lends stability to marriage because its principles and values naturally produce harmony. When put into action, Christian teaching emphasizes giving to others, self-discipline, obedience to divine commandments, conformity to the laws of man, and love and fidelity between husband and wife. When functioning as intended, marriage provides a shield against addictions to alcohol, pornography, gambling, materialism, and other behaviors that could be damaging to the relationship. Is it any wonder that a Christ-centered relationship is the best ground floor for a marriage?

Aleksandr Solzhenitsyn, that great Soviet dissident, once wrote, "If I were called upon to identify briefly the principal trait of the entire twentieth century, here too I would be unable to find anything more precise and pithy than to repeat once again: Men have forgotten God."

Don't let this happen in your home.

Persistent Prayer

If a commitment to Christ is the foundation for a successful marriage, then daily prayer together is the steady, brick-by-brick construction that provides a safe haven for genuine intimacy.

It was certainly true for my parents. James Dobson Sr. was a pastor and evangelist for most of his life. He often spent hours-long sessions on his knees, talking with God and praying for his ministry and those he loved. He was known in the small Texas town where I spent my preschool years as "the man with no leather on the toes of his shoes." He spent so much time on his knees that he wore out the toes before he did the soles!

But Dad did not only pray alone. My mother, his beloved wife, whom he called Myrt, regularly joined him to pray in times of crisis, during life's routine periods, and for occasional help and guidance in dealing with a rambunctious son named Jim. Their prayer times together must have made a deep impression on me from my earliest days, for I was told that at just one year of age I attempted to pray with them. I hadn't yet learned to talk, so I tried to imitate the sounds they were making as they communicated with God.

I have no doubt that my parents' unswerving love for Jesus Christ, renewed by daily conversation with Him, in turn cemented their own deep affection and respect for each other. Their prayer life was the glue that preserved a loving forty-three-year union that lasted until the moment my father left this earth in 1977.

I have tried to follow that example in my own home. The countless times that Shirley and I have bowed before God to offer words of thanks, petitions for assistance, and expressions of love have strengthened our relationship, too, in ways that can never be measured. Prayer has been *the* stabilizing influence for our life together.

Of course, some people use prayer the way they follow their horoscopes, attempting to manipulate an unidentified "higher power." One of my friends teasingly admits that he utters a prayer each morning on the way to work when he passes the doughnut shop. He knows it is unhealthy to eat the greasy pastries, but he loves them dearly. Therefore, he asks the Lord for permission to indulge himself each day. He'll say, "If it is Your will that I have a doughnut this morning, let there be a parking space available as I circle the block." If no spot can be found for his car, he circles the block and prays again.

Shirley and I have taken our prayer life a bit more seriously. In good times, in hard times, in moments of anxiety, and in periods of praise we have shared this wonderful privilege of talking directly to our heavenly Father. What a concept! No appointment is needed to enter into His presence. We don't have to go through His subordinates or bribe His secretaries. He is simply there, whenever we bow together before Him. Some of the highlights of my life have occurred in these quiet sessions with the Lord.

Do not misunderstand—prayer when you are alone, with a friend, in a Bible study, or in church is extremely important and valued just as much by our Father. But there is something special about prayer between husband, wife, and God that can't be found elsewhere. It creates a spiritual connection, accountability, and a holy bond that brings strength and stability to the relationship. It can even allow you to communicate about sensitive issues that might otherwise never come out—issues that can be discussed and prayed over in a spirit of humility and purity of motive.

There is something special about
prayer between husband, wife, and God.

Prayer of this kind can revitalize a marriage. In 1983, after years of discomfort and a vague sense of spiritual unrest, Christian recording artist Steve Green poured out his heart to the Lord in prayer and experienced a spiritual renewal. Just a few weeks later, his wife, Marijean, did the same thing. For the first time in their marriage, the Greens began talking to God, together, on a regular basis.

"I thought we had a good marriage before because we didn't fight, we were compatible, we enjoyed being together," Steve says. "But after our renewal, suddenly we were communicating at the deepest level. There was a bond of God's Spirit holding us and tying us together. Our relationship became a spiritual one, and it just flourished."

For the Greens, the key to unlocking these blessings was a persistent prayer life.

Intimacy with Jesus

When Shirley and I committed our lives to each other on that warm August night in Pasadena all those years ago, it was a prayer that best captured everything we would hope to be and achieve during our marriage. My father and my uncle, Rev. David L. Sharp, conducted the ceremony that evening, and it was my dad who offered these stirring words to heaven:

O eternal God: We bring Thee our children, Jimmy and Shirley. They were Thine, but Thou in love didst lend them to us for a little season to care for, to love, and to cherish. It has been a labor of love that has seemed but a few days because of the affection we bear them. Fresh from Thy hand they were in the morning of their lives. Clean and upright, but yet two separate personalities. Tonight we give them back to Thee—no longer as two—but as one flesh. *May nothing short of death dissolve the union here cemented.* And to this end let the marvelous grace of God do its perfect work!

It is also our earnest prayer for them, *not* that God shall have a part of their lives, but that He shall have the preeminent part; not that they shall possess faith, but that faith shall fully possess them both; that in a materialistic world they shall not live for the earthly and temporal alone, but that they shall be enabled to lay hold of that which is *spiritual* and *eternal.*

Let their lives together be like the course of the sun—rising in strength, going forth in power, and shining more and more unto the perfect day. Let the end of their lives resemble the setting of the sun—going down in a sea of glory, only to shine on undimmed in the firmament of a better world than this.

In the name of the Father, and of the Son, and of the Holy Ghost. Amen.

Isn't that a wonderful description of the purpose of marriage? A man and a woman are joined together as "one flesh," forever united by God's grace in a holy effort to achieve the best He has to offer—a life shining like the sun, built on love for the Lord, on a fully realized faith, and on the promise of the eternal.

If you and your mate genuinely want to experience God's best for your marriage—a relationship characterized by true love and genuine intimacy—you must face the truth about your standing before Him. According to the Bible, we are all born with a sinful nature (Romans 3:23). This sin problem prevents us from living God's way, whether as individuals or as a married couple. In fact, unresolved sin will block even your strongest efforts to have a successful marriage, because the inescapable outcome of sin is slavery to our worst impulses and—eventually—death (see Romans 6:23).

But there is a wonderful alternative! Jesus Christ paid the price for your sin through His death on the cross. And through His miraculous resurrection, He rescued you from eternal destruction. You can reach out in faith to receive your free gift of new life. Jesus put the Good News this way: "For God so loved the world that he gave his one and only Son, that whoever believes in him shall not perish but have eternal life" (John 3:16).

It really is that simple: If you choose to repent of your sin and receive the gift of salvation through faith in Jesus Christ, you *will* be forgiven and receive His gift of eternal life.

Jesus loves you and longs for fellowship with you. When you kneel before Christ and spend time with Him in prayer, you draw closer to Him and bring joy to heaven. If you do not have this kind of relationship with Jesus, I invite you to offer the following prayer tonight. Intimacy in marriage begins with intimacy with the Lord. For every human being who invites Jesus into his or her heart, *that* is the moment real life begins!

God, I am a sinner in need of You. I can't live right or hope for eternal life on my own. Please forgive my sins. I believe that Jesus Christ is Your only Son. You sent Him to die in my place and set me free from sin. Thank You!
Amen.

Establishing a Christ-Centered Home

- Have you and your mate each made the choice to receive God's gift of salvation? If not, what is keeping you from making that choice, and how can you overcome it?

- When was your last meaningful prayer time with your partner? If you're not already doing so, plan to pray together daily for the next two weeks. Talk about any changes that you see in your relationship with the Lord and with each other.

- Write down ways that you and your partner can encourage each other to spend more time in God's Word, then discuss them together.

2

A Lifelong Commitment

> *"They are no longer two, but one.*
> *Therefore what God has joined together,*
> *let man not separate."*
>
> MATTHEW 19:6

Let's return to our panel of six hundred marriage "experts." If their first recommendation for success in marriage was a Christ-centered home, what was second on their list?

It was yet another back-to-basics concept—namely, committed love. These couples had lived long enough to know that a weak marital commitment usually leads to divorce. One participant wrote:

> Marriage is no fairy-tale land of enchantment. But you can create an oasis of love in the midst of a harsh world by grinding it out and sticking in there.

Another said:

> Perfection doesn't exist. You have to approach the first few years of marriage with a learner's permit to work out your incompatibilities. It is a continual effort.

Those views don't sound particularly romantic, do they? But they do carry the wisdom of experience. Two people are not compatible simply because they love each other and are both professing Christians. Many young people assume that the sunshine and flowers that characterized their courtship will continue for the rest of their lives. Don't you believe it! It is naïve to expect two unique and strong-willed individuals to fit together easily like a couple of machines. Even gears have multiple cogs with rough edges that must be honed before they will work in concert.

That honing process usually occurs in the first years of marriage. What often happens at this time is a dramatic struggle for power in the relationship. Who will lead? Who will follow? Who will determine how the money is spent? Who will get his way or her way in times of disagreement? Everything is up for grabs in the beginning, and the way these early decisions are made will set the stage for the future.

If both partners come into the relationship prepared for battle, the foundation will begin to crumble.

Therein lies the danger. Abraham Lincoln said, quoting the Lord Jesus, "A house divided against itself cannot stand" (see Mark 3:25). If both partners come into the relationship prepared for battle, the foundation will begin to crumble. The apostle Paul gave us the divine perspective on human relationships—not only in marriage but in every dimension of life. He wrote, "Do nothing out of selfish ambition or vain conceit, but in humility consider others better than yourselves" (Philippians 2:3).

That one verse contains more wisdom than most marriage manuals combined. If heeded, it could virtually eliminate divorce from the catalog of human experience—no small achievement, considering that more than one million marriages break apart in the United States every year.[1] If you want yours to be different, I urge you to commit now to "sticking in there" during the newlywed phase, the middle years, and your golden age together.

Persisting Through the Pain

I can commend no better model of selfless, unconditional commitment than Robertson McQuilkin. In his book *A Promise Kept*, he relates how he served as president of a thriving seminary and Bible college in South Carolina for more than twenty years. His wife, Muriel, supported him in many ways, including as an excellent cook and hostess when they entertained guests of the college in their home. They were an effective ministry team.

Then Muriel's health declined. Tests confirmed her doctor's fears: She had Alzheimer's disease. In time, Muriel's abilities failed and Robertson became increasingly responsible for her basic needs, which included feeding, bathing, and dressing his wife.

With Muriel's needs escalating and his duties at the college unchanged, Robertson faced a difficult decision: Should he place Muriel in an institution? He loved his work and felt that God had called him to service as a college president. Yet he also knew that putting God first in his life meant that "all the responsibilities He gives are first too." Decades ago, Robertson had made a promise before the Lord to love, cherish, and care for Muriel, and he knew that God expected him to continue to honor that promise. Ultimately, the decision proved an easy one. Robertson resigned from his position so that he could better care for Muriel. It was his turn to humbly serve his wife.[2]

Unlike so many people today, Robertson McQuilkin clearly understood the meaning of *commitment*. As his wife's mind and body deteriorated with no hope for a cure, he willingly abandoned the work and ministry he enjoyed and had worked so hard to build. Muriel needed him, and he would be there for her, even though she could give him nothing back—not even a rational "thank you." This, in all its magnificence—and sorrow—is the meaning of love.

Very few certainties touch us all in this mortal existence, but one absolute is that, like the McQuilkins, we too will experience hardship and stress. Nobody remains unscathed. Life will test each of us severely, if not during our younger years, then through the events surrounding our final days. Jesus spoke of this inevitability when He said to His disciples, "In the world ye shall have tribulation: but be of good cheer; I have overcome the world" (John 16:33, KJV).

My pastor put it this way: "There are two categories of people in the world—those who are suffering, and those who *will* suffer."

Dr. Richard Selzer is a surgeon who has written several outstanding books about his beloved patients, including *Mortal Lessons* and *Letters to a Young Doctor*. In the first of these texts, he describes the experience of "horror" that invades one's life sooner or later. When we're young, he says, we seem to be shielded from it the way the body is protected against bacterial infection. Microscopic organisms are all around us, yet our bodies' defenses effectually hold them at bay—at least for a season. Likewise, each day we walk in and through a world of horror unscathed, as though surrounded by an impenetrable membrane of protection. We may even be unaware that distressing possibilities exist during the period of youthful good health. But then one day, without warning, the membrane tears and horror seeps into our lives. Until that moment, it was always someone else's misfortune—another man's tragedy—and not our own. The tearing of the membrane can be devastating, especially for those who do not know the "good cheer" Jesus gives in times of tribulation.

Having served on a large medical school faculty for fourteen years, I watched husbands and wives in the hours when horror began to penetrate the protective membrane. All too commonly, their marital relationships were shattered by the new stresses that invaded their lives. Parents of a mentally retarded child, for example, often blamed one another for the tragedy that confronted them. Instead of clinging to each other in love and reassurance, they added to their sorrows by attacking each other. I do not condemn them for this human failing, but I do pity them for it. A basic ingredient was missing in their relationship, which remained unrecognized until the membrane tore: It was the essential component of commitment.

A number of years ago, I heard the late Dr. Francis Schaeffer speak to this issue. He described the bridges in Europe built by the Romans in the first and second centuries AD. They are still standing today, despite being constructed of unreinforced brick and mortar. Why haven't they collapsed in this modern era of heavy trucks and equipment? The reason they remain intact is because they are used for nothing but foot traffic. If an eighteen-wheel semi were driven across the historic structures, they would crumble in a great cloud of dust and debris.

Marriages that lack an iron-willed determination to hang together at all costs are like those fragile Roman bridges. They appear to be secure and may indeed remain upright—until they are put under heavy pressure. That's when the seams split and the foundation crumbles. It appears to me that the majority of young couples today are in that incredibly vulnerable position. Their relationships are constructed of unreinforced mud that will not withstand the weighty trials lying ahead. The determination to survive together simply is not there.

What, then, will you do when unexpected crises descend upon your home, or when your marriage seems limp and lifeless? Will you pack it in? Will you pout and cry and seek ways to strike back? Or will your commitment hold steady? These questions must be addressed *now*, before Satan has an opportunity to put his noose of discouragement around your neck. Set your jaw and clench your fists. Nothing short of death must ever be permitted to come between the two of you. *Nothing!*

Emotions: You Can't Trust Them

A loving commitment, so critical to the success of any marriage, is needed not only for the great tragedies of life, but also for the daily frustrations that wear and tear on a relationship. These minor irritants, when accumulated over time, may be even more threatening to a relationship than catastrophic events. And yes, Virginia, there are times in every good marriage when a husband and wife don't like each other very much. There are even occasions when they feel as though they will never love their partner again.

The problem lies in that word *feel.* The *feeling* of love is simply too ephemeral to hold a relationship together for very long. It comes and goes. Emotions are like that. They flatten out occasionally, like an automobile tire with a nail in the tread—riding on the rim is a pretty bumpy experience for everyone on board.

The feeling of love is simply too ephemeral to hold a relationship together for very long.

The fickleness of emotions reminds me of the joke about the wedding of a young contract lawyer and his bride. When the minister came to the vows, he intoned, "Do you take this woman for better? For worse? For richer? For poorer? In sickness? And in health?"

He was startled to hear the groom reply, "Yes. No. Yes. No. No. And yes."

In another wedding ceremony, this one real, the bride and groom pledged to stay married as long as they *continued to love each other*. Let's hope they both have good divorce attorneys, because they're going to need them. Relationships based on feelings are necessarily transitory. Emotions are, in fact, inveterate liars that will often confirm our worst fears in the absence of supporting evidence. Even the young and the brave can be fooled by the shenanigans of runaway emotions.

I am not denying the importance of feelings in our human relationships. Indeed, those who have so insulated themselves that they no longer feel are very unhealthy individuals. But we must understand that emotions are unreliable and, at times, tyrannical. They should never be permitted to dominate us.

That principle has generally been understood since the days of Scripture. We read in 2 Corinthians 10:5, "Take captive every thought to make it obedient to Christ." That's pretty clear, isn't it? And consider Galatians 5:22: "But when the Holy Spirit controls our lives he will produce this kind of fruit in us: love, joy, peace, patience, kindness, goodness, faithfulness, gentleness and self-control" (TLB). These are called *the fruits of the Spirit*, and they begin with the attribute listed last—the exercise of self-control.

One of the evidences of emotional and spiritual maturity is the ability (and the willingness) to overrule ephemeral feelings and govern our behavior with reason. This might lead you to tough it out when you feel like escaping; and guard your tongue when you feel like shouting; and to save your money when you feel like spending it; and to remain faithful when you feel like flirting; and to put the welfare of your mate above your own. These are mature acts that can't occur when biased, whimsical, and unreliable feelings are in charge. Emotions are important in a relationship, to be sure, but they must be supported by the will and a lifetime commitment.

I once attempted to express this thought to my wife on an anniversary card:

To My Darlin' Little Wife, Shirley, on the Occasion of Our Eighth Anniversary

I'm sure you remember the many, many occasions during our eight years of marriage when the tide of love and affection soared high above the crest...times when our feeling for each other was almost limitless. This kind of intense emotion can't be brought about voluntarily, but it often accompanies a time of particular happiness. We felt it when I was offered my first professional position. We felt it when the world's most precious child came home from the maternity ward of Huntington Hospital. We felt it when the University of Southern California chose to award a doctoral degree to me. But emotions are strange! We felt the same closeness when the opposite kind of event took place; when threat and potential disaster

41

entered our lives. We felt an intense closeness when a medical problem threatened to postpone our marriage plans. We felt it when you were hospitalized last year. I felt it intensely when I knelt over your unconscious form after a grinding automobile accident.

I'm trying to say this: Both happiness and threat bring that overwhelming appreciation and affection for our beloved sweethearts. But the fact is, most of life is made up of neither disaster nor unusual hilarity. Rather, it is composed of the routine, calm, everyday events in which we participate. And during these times, I enjoy the quiet, serene love that actually surpasses the effervescent display, in many ways. It is not as exuberant, perhaps, but it runs deep and solid. I find myself firmly in that kind of love on this Eighth Anniversary. Today I feel the steady and quiet affection that comes from a devoted heart. I am committed to you and your happiness, more now than I've ever been. I want to remain your "sweetheart."

When events throw us together emotionally, we will enjoy the thrill and romantic excitement. But during life's routine, like today, my love stands undiminished. Happy Anniversary to my wonderful wife.

Your Jim

"I Promise..."

Love can be defined in myriad ways, but in marriage "I love you" really means: "I promise to be there for you all of my days." It is a promise that says, "I'll be there when you lose your job, your health, your parents, your looks, your confidence, your friends." It's a promise that tells your partner, "I'll build you up; I'll overlook your weaknesses; I'll forgive your mistakes; I'll put your needs above my own; I'll stick by you even when the going gets tough."

This kind of assurance will hold you steady through all of life's ups and downs, through all the "better or worse" conditions. When you follow through on the promise of "I love you," it is the fulfillment of our Lord's instruction in Scripture: "Simply let your 'Yes' be 'Yes,' and your 'No,' 'No'" (Matthew 5:37).

"I love you" really means: "I promise to be there for you all of my days."

Our heavenly Father has demonstrated throughout the ages that He keeps His promises, including the most important one of all: reserving a spot in heaven for each of His followers, for all eternity. Since God keeps His promises, we must keep ours, too—especially the one we made before God, our family, our friends, and our church on our wedding day.

I hope you'll indulge me as I share a few more words presented by a man expressing this kind of commitment to a woman. Seventy years ago my father, James Dobson Sr., spoke these words to his fiancée (my future mother) after she agreed to become his wife:

I want you to understand and be fully aware of my feelings concerning the marriage covenant we are about to enter. I have been taught at my mother's knee, in harmony with the Word of God, that the marriage vows are inviolable, and by entering into them I am binding myself absolutely and for life. The idea of estrangement from you through divorce for any reason at all [although God allows one—infidelity] will never at any time be permitted to enter into my thinking. I'm not naïve in this. On the contrary, I'm fully aware of the possibility, unlikely as it now appears, that mutual incompatibility or other unforeseen circumstances could result in extreme mental suffering. If such becomes the case, I am resolved for my part to accept it as a consequence of the commitment I am now making and to bear it, if necessary, to the end of our lives together.

I have loved you dearly as a sweetheart

and will continue to love you as my wife. But over and above that, I love you with a Christian love that demands that I never react in any way toward you that would jeopardize our prospects of entering heaven, which is the supreme objective of both our lives. And I pray that God Himself will make our affection for one another perfect and eternal.

James and Myrtle Dobson enjoyed a loving, committed, fulfilling marriage that began in 1935 and ended with his death in 1977. They never wavered for a moment through all those years. If you approach your own marriage with this determination, you too will establish a stable, rewarding relationship that will last a lifetime.

Your commitment to each other will do even more than enable your marriage to go the distance. It will establish the essential foundation of trust that is a requirement for true intimacy in any relationship. We'll talk more about trust in the chapter ahead.

Cultivating Committed Love

- What role do emotions play in your relationship with your partner? Talk about this together, then reaffirm your commitment to each other, regardless of your feelings at any given time.

- Identify another couple whose marriage has stayed secure under stress. Ask them, "What is your secret?" Decide if their methods can also be applied to your marriage.

- Reread the statement made by James Dobson Sr. to his fiancée. Get together with your partner and renew in writing your lifetime commitment to each other.

A Deep and Abiding Trust

Love...always trusts.

1 Corinthians 13:6-7

From the start of a relationship, and certainly throughout marriage, each of us faces a critical question on a daily basis: Do I trust my partner or not? We may not even be aware that the question is before us, but even so, the way we answer it has everything to do with the level of intimacy we ultimately achieve with our mate. Relationships dominated by fear and insecurity will never reach their potential, but marriages founded on trust and safety will flourish.

At one time or another, most of us have felt some anxiety about our spouse's commitment, whether from a genuine threat to the relationship or because of our own insecurities and imaginings. Even as Christians, we know that we can place unequivocal confidence in the Lord. But absolute, unquestioned trust in our spouse? That can be harder to bestow. The truth is, it must be earned over time—word by word, deed by deed.

Building Trust with Words

Do you enjoy teasing your husband or wife? When you're with friends, do you occasionally reveal an embarrassing secret about him or her?

One key to building trust is to take great care not to hurt or embarrass those we love. Some information is private and should remain so. For one partner to reveal family secrets indiscriminately or to verbalize barely concealed put-downs breaks the couple's bond of loyalty and violates trust.

If you have ever been to a party and watched someone play "Assassinate the Spouse," you know what I mean. The objective is simple: A contestant attempts to punish his mate by ridiculing her in front of their friends. If he wants to be especially vicious, he lets the guests know he thinks she is dumb and ugly. It's a brutal game with no winners. The contest ends when his wife is totally divested of self-respect and dignity; he gets bonus points if he can reduce her to tears.

Sound cruel? It is, even when it's carried out under the guise of joking or teasing. It's never enjoyable to watch someone take out anger against his (or her) mate in this way. We're most sensitive to the comments of our mates in the presence of our peers. This is a word game that should never be played.

Also beware of another type of charade: using your "sharing" with your spouse to create insecurity and gain power over him or her. I know of a handsome young company president who told his wife every day about the single women at the office who flirted with him. His candor was admirable, but by not *also* stressing his commitment to his wife, he was saying (consciously or not): "You'd better treat me right because there are plenty of women out there just waiting to get their hands on me." His wife began to fret about how she could hang onto her husband.

He should have reflected on his real motives for alarming his wife. Did this kind of sharing nurture or injure his friendship and trust with her? And she could have helped redirect the conversations by pointing out to her husband—in a calm, nonthreatening manner—how his words made her feel.

Building Trust with Actions

Words and the way you use them are terribly significant, but the surest way to establish trust in marriage is through your actions. Build a record of choices and deeds that proves to your partner you can be trusted at all times—especially in regards to your relations with the opposite sex.

Build a record of choices and deeds that proves to your partner you can be trusted at all times.

For my own part, I can honestly say that I have never considered cheating on Shirley. The very thought of hurting her and inviting God's wrath are more than enough to keep me on the straight and narrow. Furthermore, I would never destroy the specialness that we have shared for all these years. But even in marriages that are based on that kind of commitment, Satan will try to undermine them.

He laid a trap for me during a time of particular vulnerability. Shirley and I had been married just a few years when we had a minor fuss. It was no big deal, but we both were pretty agitated at the time. I got in the car and drove around for about an hour to cool off. Then when I was on the way home, a very attractive girl drove up beside me in her car and smiled. She was obviously flirting with me. Then she slowed down, looked back, and turned onto a side street. I knew she was inviting me to follow her.

I didn't take the bait. I just went on home and made up with Shirley. But I thought later about how vicious Satan had been to take advantage of the momentary conflict between us. Scripture refers to the devil as "a roaring lion…seeking whom he may devour" (1 Peter 5:8, KJV). I can see how true that description really is. He knew his best opportunity to damage our marriage was during that hour or two when we were irritated with each other. That is typical of his strategy. He'll lay a trap for you, too, and it'll probably come at a time of vulnerability. Beautiful, enticing, forbidden fruit will be offered to you when your "hunger" is greatest. If you are foolish enough to reach for it, your fingers will sink into rotten mush on the back side. That's the way sin operates in our lives. It promises everything; it delivers nothing but disgust and heartache.

Someone said it this way: All you need to grow the finest crop of weeds is a tiny crack in your sidewalk.

Hedges Around Your Home

How, then, can we keep cracks from developing in the sidewalks of our marriages? Well, the surest way to avoid an affair is to flee temptation as soon as it confronts you. Author Jerry Jenkins has referred to this determination to preserve moral purity as "building hedges" around marriage so that temptation is never given a foothold. You take steps to protect yourself and enhance the level of trust in your marriage at the same time.

To build a hedge around your home, talk with your partner about your interactions with the opposite sex; then establish sensible, sensitive guidelines. Some couples rule out lunch with a coworker, traveling together, talking alone behind closed doors, sharing rides, or working as a "couple" on a project. Agree on what you both consider reasonable, then stick to that agreement. If you're faced with a situation that you haven't discussed, ask your spouse about it beforehand, and if he or she isn't comfortable with it, don't do it. *Listen* to each other's concerns. The Lord has made you "one flesh" for good reason.

It may be harmless to show a bit of friendliness to a member of the opposite sex, but avoid crossing the line into flirting. Ask yourself, *Would my spouse feel comfortable if he or she witnessed this exchange? Would my actions earn trust, or would they raise doubt about my motives?*

At first it may seem strange to ask for permission to take part in what's probably a completely innocent activity. But you'll quickly discover how wonderfully reassuring it feels when the situation is reversed and your partner is the one asking you!

Watch for warning signs that you may be vulnerable to an affair. Dr. Merville Vincent once wrote an article for the *Christian Medical Society Journal* describing how doctors, or anyone in a position of authority, can fall into temptation's trap.[3] In Dr. Vincent's scenario, an unhappily married or divorced young woman visits her physician for treatment of a medical problem. The woman may feel frightened and helpless. The doctor, on the other hand, seems strong, confident, and caring and is able to solve her immediate problem. The woman believes the doctor is wonderful and tells him so. He immediately concurs.

The doctor, meanwhile, has his own problems at home. Perhaps because of the hours he spends at work, his desire to be cared for is not being met by his wife, who may herself be tired of trying to give to this man who makes little attempt to meet *her* needs for an involved husband and father of her children. She puts more demands on him at home; he feels underappreciated. Suddenly, his young patient begins to look increasingly attractive.

It is a recipe for disaster. The first warning sign is when the husband (or wife) begins to feel that his patient (or client or coworker) appreciates him and loves him more than his spouse and family do. The next sign is when the husband (or wife) finds ways to spend more time with his new interest and less time at home. At that point, an affair is only a step away.

According to Dr. Vincent, this predicament can be prevented if couples realize that infidelity develops out of unmet needs—the husband's, the wife's, and a third party's. They should realize that meeting dependent needs with an erotic response makes the situation worse, not better. They should also understand that a sure way to prevent an affair is for a husband and wife to *both* put the other's needs ahead of their own. I agree. An attitude of service and sacrifice is an indisputable marriage builder.

One final caution regarding temptation: I urge you to be wary of pride in your own infallibility. The minute you begin thinking that an affair "would never happen to me" is when you become most vulnerable. We are sexual creatures with powerful urges. We are also fallen beings with strong desires to do wrong. That is what temptation is all about. Do *not* give it a place in your life. My father once wrote, "Strong desire is like a powerful river. As long as it stays within the banks of God's will, all will be proper and clean. But when it overflows those boundaries, devastation awaits downstream."

Some time ago I discovered a little recognized, but universal, characteristic of human nature: *We value that which we are fortunate to get; we discredit that with which we are stuck! We lust for the very thing which is beyond our grasp; we disdain that same item when it becomes a permanent possession.*[4] This helps explain the incredible power that the lure of infidelity can have on our behavior. Nevertheless, God promises to provide a "way out" of temptation if we will look for it (1 Corinthians 10:13). Keep looking for the way out and you'll keep building up trust in your marriage.

Trust Begins with God

Of course, even in the best of marriages, it is possible for husbands and wives to err and break the other's trust. That is why we *must* rely on God's power—not our own—if we hope to achieve an intimate marriage. It is only when husbands and wives commit themselves to living according to God's ways that a deep and lasting bond of trust develops between them. We can give our heart confidently to our spouse when we know that he or she is genuinely seeking to follow God and His guidelines.

Only confidence in God's faithfulness gives us the courage to remain vulnerably open, knowing that we might be hurt. In the 1993 movie *Shadowlands*, writer C. S. Lewis loved a woman who died prematurely. Her death was intensely painful to him, causing Lewis to question whether he should have permitted himself to care for her. He concluded in the last scene that we are given two choices in life. We can allow ourselves to love and care for others, which makes us vulnerable to their sickness, death, or rejection. Or we can protect ourselves by refusing to love.

Lewis decided that it is better to feel and to suffer than to go through life isolated, insulated, and lonely. I agree strongly.

Yes, trusting your mate is risky. But the fulfillment of genuine intimacy makes the risk worthwhile.

Building Trust Together

- How deep is your trust in God? How much do you trust your partner? Talk together about how trust in the Lord can build trust in your marriage.

- Do you understand how strongly God feels about adultery? Read Exodus 20:14; Leviticus 18:20, 20:10; Proverbs 7; Malachi 3:5; Matthew 5:27–28; Mark 10:11–12; John 8:1–11; Romans 7:2–3; Ephesians 5:3–5; and Hebrews 13:4.

- Are you and your spouse both comfortable with each other's behavior around the opposite sex? Talk about guidelines that you can both agree on that will build hedges around your home.

4

A Willingness to Communicate

*Each of you should look not only to your own
interests, but also to the interests of others.*

PHILIPPIANS 2:4

The art of communication doesn't come naturally to most of us. Some folks just don't like
to talk much. Others talk incessantly without
ever really saying anything. But when it comes to
marriage, communication is one of *the* keys to
intimacy. Those who master this skill are likely to
enjoy a close, fulfilling, productive relationship.
Those who continually fail to understand each

other, however, often feel isolated and alone. This is a major contributor to divorce.

One of the primary reasons for communication troubles in marriage is a fundamental difference between males and females. Research makes it clear that most little girls are blessed with greater linguistic ability than most little boys, and it remains a lifelong talent. Simply stated, she talks more than he does. As an adult, she typically expresses her feelings and thoughts far better than her husband and is often irritated by his reticence. God may have given her 50,000 words per day, and her husband only 25,000. (Or maybe it only seems that way.) He comes home from work with 24,975 used up and merely grunts his way through the evening. He may descend into Monday night football while his wife is dying to expend her remaining 25,000 words. A female columnist, commenting on this male tendency, even proposed that an ordinance be passed stating that a man who watches 168,000 football games in a single season be declared legally dead. (All in favor say, "Aye.")

The complexity of the human personality guarantees exceptions to every generalization. Yet any knowledgeable marriage counselor knows that the inability or unwillingness of husbands to reveal their feelings to their wives is one of the common complaints of women. It can almost be stated as an absolute: Show me a quiet, reserved husband, and I'll show you a frustrated wife. She wants to know what he's thinking, what happened at the office or job site, how he views the children, and especially, how he feels about her. The husband, by contrast, finds some things better left unsaid. It is a classic struggle.

The paradox is that a highly emotional, verbal woman is sometimes drawn to the strong, silent type. He seemed so secure and "in control" before they were married. She admired his unflappable nature and his coolness in a crisis. Then they were married and the flip side of his great strength became obvious: He wouldn't talk! So for the next forty years, she gnashed her teeth because her husband couldn't give what she needed from him. It just wasn't in him.

I once received the letter below (modified to protect the identity of the writer) which represents a thousand others I've received:

Dear Dr. Dobson:

I have read your book *What Wives Wish Their Husbands Knew About Women.* Unfortunately, I couldn't get my husband to read your book, which brings me to my problem. It is really hard to communicate with my husband when I have to compete with the television, kids, and work. At mealtimes, which should be a time for talking, he has to listen to Paul Harvey news on the radio. He's not home for the evening meal because he works the 3 to 11 p.m. shift. I really would like him to listen to your *Focus on the Family* program, but he won't...

Another woman handed me the following note after hearing me speak. It says in a few words what others conveyed with many:

Will you *please* discuss this. [My husband] arrives home, reads the newspaper, eats dinner, talks on the phone, watches TV, takes a shower, and goes to bed. This is a *constant daily routine.* It never changes. On Sunday we go to church, then come home. We take a nap and then it's back to work again on Monday morning. Our daughter is nine, and we are not communicating, and life is speeding by in this monotonous routine.

I can hear some of you saying, "If women want more time set aside for talking and sharing with their husbands, why don't they just tell them so?" They *do* tell them so, in fact. But husbands (and occasionally wives) often find it very difficult to "hear" this message.

I'm reminded of the night my father was preaching in an open tent service which was attended by more cats and dogs than people. During the course of his sermon, one large alley cat decided to take a nap on the platform. Inevitably, my father took a step backward and planted his heel squarely on the tail of the tom. The cat literally went crazy, scratching and clawing to free his tail from my father's six-foot, three-inch frame. But Dad could become very preoccupied while preaching, and he didn't notice the disturbance. There at his feet was a panicky animal, digging holes in the carpet and screaming for mercy, yet the heel did not move. Dad later said he thought the screech came from the brakes of automobiles at a nearby corner. When my father finally walked off the cat's tail, still unaware of the commotion, the tom took off like a Saturn rocket.

This story typifies many modern marriages. The wife is screaming and clawing the air and writhing in pain, but the husband is oblivious to her panic. He is preoccupied with his own thoughts, not realizing that a single step to the left or right could alleviate the crisis. I never cease to be amazed at just how deaf a man can become under these circumstances.

Marriage Misconceptions

Related to this bewildering dilemma—a mate who neither speaks nor hears—is another common problem that has its origins in childhood. Girls are subtly taught by our culture that marriage is a life-long romantic experience; that loving husbands are entirely responsible for the happiness of their wives; that a good relationship between a man and a woman should be sufficient to meet all needs and desires; and that any sadness or depression that a woman might encounter is her husband's fault. Or at least he has the power to eradicate it if he cares enough. In other words, many American women come into marriage with unrealistically romantic expectations which are certain to be dashed. Not only does this orientation set up a bride for disappointment and agitation in the future, but it also places enormous pressure on her husband to deliver the impossible.

Unfortunately, the man of the house was taught some misconceptions in his formative years, too. He learned, perhaps from his father, that his only responsibility is to provide materially for his family. He must enter a business or profession and succeed at all costs, climbing the ladder of success and achieving an ever-increasing standard of living as proof of manhood. It never occurs to him that he is supposed to "carry" his wife emotionally. For Pete's sake! If he pays his family's bills and is a loyal husband, what more could any woman ask for? He simply doesn't understand what she wants.

Inevitably, these differing assumptions collide

head-on during the early years of marriage. Young John is out there competing like crazy in the marketplace, thinking his successes are automatically appreciated by his wife. To his shock, she not only fails to notice, but even seems to resent the work that takes him from her. "I'm doing it for you, babe!" he says. Diane isn't convinced.

At first, John tries to accommodate Diane. At other times, he becomes angry and they slug it out in a verbal brawl. The following morning, he feels terrible about these fights. Gradually, his personality begins to change. He hates conflict with his wife and withdraws as a means of avoidance. What he needs most from his home (like the majority of men) is *tranquility*. Thus, he finds ways of escaping. He reads the paper, watches television, works in his shop, goes fishing, cuts the grass, plays golf, works at his desk, goes to a ball game—anything to stay out of the way of his hostile wife. Does this pacify her? Not even close! It is even more infuriating to have one's anger ignored.

Here she is, screaming for attention and venting her hostility for his husbandly failures. And what does he do in return? He hides. He becomes more silent. He runs. The cycle has become a vicious one. The more anger she displays over his uninvolvement, the more detached he becomes. This inflames his wife with even greater hostility. She has said everything there is to say and it produced no response. Now she feels powerless and disrespected. Every morning he goes off to work where he can socialize with his friends, but she is stuck in this state of emotional deprivation.

Of course, if both spouses work or if the wife is the family breadwinner, then the dynamics of the situation are changed. But the fundamental need for sharing and intimacy in marriage—especially for the wife—remain. Regardless of the circumstances, if one partner feels neglected over a long period of time, she may begin looking for ways to hurt her spouse in return. When a relationship has deteriorated to this point, the idea of intimacy with one's mate seems as foreign as a visitor from Mars.

I know that I have painted a bleak picture of the all-too-common ways that communication can break down in marriages. But if you recognize yourself in any of the scenarios above, do not give up hope! Each of us can improve communication in his or her relationship by turning to a variety of time-honored solutions.

Restoring the Information Flow

For the man and wife who find that the flow of information between them is blocked, compromise is in order. Even a naturally reticent man has a clear responsibility to "cheer up his wife which he hath taken" (Deuteronomy 24:5, KJV). He must not claim himself a "rock" who will never allow himself to be vulnerable again. Instead, he must press himself to open his heart and share his deeper feelings with his wife. Time must be reserved for meaningful conversations. Taking walks, going out to breakfast, or riding bicycles on a Saturday morning are fresh opportunities for conversation that can help keep love alive. Communication can occur even in families where the husband leans inward and the wife leans outward. In these instances, I believe that the primary responsibility for compromise lies with the husband.

Your sharing must sometimes extend to difficult subjects. If you're in charge of the family finances, and you've accidentally or foolishly depleted the bank account, don't hide it—let your spouse know. If someone makes a pass at you at work, tell your partner, even if it's uncomfortable to do so. As you work together to find the best solution for problems like these, you'll grow closer.

Time must be reserved for meaningful conversations.

If you reveal your inner feelings honestly, with pure motives, and continually reaffirm your commitment to your marriage, your spouse will become your most treasured confidante, protector, adviser, and friend.

An extremely useful technique for couples seeking to improve their communication is the word picture, described by Gary Smalley and John Trent in their book *The Language of Love*. In one of their examples, a high school teacher and football coach named Jim came home each evening too tired to even talk to his wife, Susan, leaving her frustrated and angry. Finally, Susan told Jim a story about a man who went to breakfast with his fellow coaches. The man ate his favorite omelet, then gathered up some crumbs and put them in a bag. Then he went to lunch with more friends and ate a turkey tenderloin pie and a huge salad. Again, he put a few crumbs in a doggie bag to take with him. When he came home that night, he handed his wife and their two boys the little bags of leftovers.

"That's the way I feel when you come home with nothing left to give," Susan said. "All we get are leftovers. I'm waiting to enjoy a meal with you, hoping for a time to talk and laugh and get to know you, longing to communicate with you the way you do every day with the guys. But all we get are doggie bags. Honey, don't you see? We don't need leftovers. We need you."

Susan's word picture brought tears to Jim's eyes and led to positive changes in their marriage.[5] You, too, may find that a graphic word picture is more effective at getting your mate's attention than a torrent of hostile words.

Another communication tool advocated by author-counselors Chuck and Barb Snyder is "quick listening,"[6] based on the following Scripture passage: "Everyone should be quick to listen, slow to speak and slow to become angry" (James 1:19).

After a disagreement, a husband and wife sit down together and explain their feelings about the issue. The catch is that the other spouse can't interrupt. Partners may try this and still disagree, but by giving their opinion and fully listening to their mate's, they'll increase their chances of understanding each other—and of staying best friends.

Happiness is a marvelous magnet to the human personality.

For the wife who finds herself attacking an unresponsive man and driving him away, there is a method of drawing him in your direction. It is accomplished by taking the pressure off him. By pulling backward a bit. By avoiding the worn-out accusations and complaints. By showing appreciation for what he does right and for being fun to be with. Happiness is a marvelous magnet to the human personality.

Sometimes it is necessary to interject a certain "mystery" into the relationship in order to attract a disengaged spouse. A demeanor of self-confidence and independence is far more effective in getting attention than a frontal assault.

I remember counseling a bright young lady whom I'll call Janet. She came to me because she seemed to be losing the affection of her husband. Frank appeared bored when he was at home, and he refused to take her out with him. On weekends, he went sailing with his friends despite the bitter protests of his wife. She had begged for his attention for months, but the slippage continued.

I hypothesized that Janet was invading Frank's territory and needed to recapture the challenge that made him want to marry her in the first place. Thus, I suggested that she retreat into her own world: stop "reaching" for him when he was at home, schedule some personal activities independently of his availability, etc. Simultaneously, I urged her to give him vague explanations about why her personality had changed. She was instructed not to display anger or discontent, allowing Frank to draw his own conclusions about what she was thinking. My purpose was to change his frame of reference. Instead of his thinking, *How can I escape from this woman who is driving me crazy?* I wanted him to wonder, *What's going on? Am I losing Janet? Have I pushed her too far? Has she found someone else?*

The results were dramatic. About a week after the change of manner was instituted, Janet and Frank were at home together one evening. After several hours of uninspired conversation and yawns, Janet told her husband that she was rather tired and wanted to go to bed. She said good-night matter-of-factly and went to her bedroom. About thirty minutes later, Frank threw open the door and turned on the light. He proceeded to make passionate love to her, later saying that he couldn't stand the barrier that had come between them. It was precisely the barrier that Janet had complained about for months. Her approach had been so over-bearing that she was driving him away from her. When she changed her direction, Frank also threw his truck in reverse. It often happens that way.

Accept the Unresolvables

Even if all of these communication techniques are employed, however, some people—usually wives—

will discover that they are married to a mate who will never be able to fully express himself or understand the needs that I have described. His emotional structure makes it impossible for him to comprehend the feelings and frustrations of another—particularly those occurring in the opposite sex. This husband will not read a book such as this and would probably resent it if he did. He has never been required to "give" and has no idea how it is done. What, then, is to be the reaction of his wife? What will you do if your husband lacks the insight to be what you need him to be?

My advice is that you change what can be altered, explain that which can be understood, teach that which can be learned, revise that which can be improved, resolve that which can be settled, and negotiate that which is open to compromise. Create the best marriage possible from the raw materials brought by two imperfect human beings with two distinctly unique personalities. But for all the rough edges that can never be smoothed and the faults that can never be eradicated, try to develop the best possible perspective and determine in your mind to accept reality exactly as it is. The first principle of mental health is to accept that which cannot be changed. You could easily go to pieces over adverse circumstances that are beyond your control. You can determine to hang tough, or you can yield to cowardice. Depression is often evidence of emotional surrender.

Someone wrote:

> Life can't give me joy and peace;
> it's up to me to will it.
> Life just gives me time and space,
> it's up to me to fill it.

Can you accept the fact that your husband will never be able to meet all your needs and aspirations? Seldom does one human being satisfy every longing and hope in another. Obviously, this coin has two sides: You can't be his perfect woman either. He is no more equipped to resolve your entire package of emotional needs than you are to become his sexual dream machine every twenty-four hours. Both partners have to settle for human foibles and faults and irritability and fatigue and occasional nighttime "headaches." A good marriage is not one in which perfection reigns; it is a relationship in which a healthy perspective overlooks a multitude of unresolvables. Thank goodness my wife, Shirley, has adopted this attitude toward me!

Seeking to Understand

- In what ways do you and your partner communicate well? In what ways do you struggle? Talk about how you both can compromise in order to improve communication in your marriage.

- Are you the victim of any "marriage misconceptions"? How has this affected your relationship with your spouse, and what can you do about it?

- Have you taken a long look at any communication difficulties in your marriage from your mate's point of view? Decide what you can do on your own to improve your situation—and if there are some realities that must be accepted as they are.

An Understanding of Love

> *Love…burns like blazing fire,*
> *like a mighty flame.*
>
> <small>SONG OF SONGS 8:6</small>

I will never forget the first Valentine's Day of my marriage, six months after Shirley and I walked down the aisle. It was something of a disaster. I had gone to the USC library that morning and spent eight or ten hours poring over dusty books and journals. It had slipped my mind completely that it was February 14.

What was worse, I was oblivious to the preparations that were going on at home. Shirley had cooked a wonderful dinner, baked a pink heart-shaped cake with "Happy Valentine's Day" written on the top, placed several red candles on the table, wrapped a small gift she had bought for me, and written a little love note on a greeting card. The stage was set. She would meet me at the front door with a kiss and a hug. But there I sat on the other side of Los Angeles, blissfully unaware of the storm gathering overhead.

About 8 p.m., I got hungry and ordered a hamburger at the University Grill. After eating, I moseyed out to where my Volkswagen was parked and headed toward home. Then I made a terrible mistake that I would regret for many moons: I stopped by to see my parents, who lived near the freeway. Mom greeted me warmly and served up a great slice of apple pie. That sealed my doom.

When I finally put my key in the lock at 10:00, I knew instantly that something was horribly wrong. (I'm very perceptive about subtleties like that.) The apartment was dark and all was deathly quiet. There on the table was a coagulated dinner still sitting in our best dishes and bowls. Half-burned candles stood cold and dark in their silver-plated holders. It appeared that I had forgotten something important. But what? Then I noticed the red and white decorations on the table. *Oh no!* I thought.

So there I stood in the semidarkness of our little living room, feeling like a creep. I didn't even have a Valentine's Day card, much less a thoughtful gift, for Shirley. No romantic thoughts had crossed my mind all day. I couldn't even pretend to want the dried-up food that sat before me. After a brief flurry of words and a few tears, Shirley went to bed and pulled the covers up around her ears. I would have given a thousand dollars for a true, plausible explanation for my thoughtlessness. But there just wasn't one. It didn't help to tell her, "I stopped by my mom's house for a piece of great apple pie. It was wonderful. You should've been there."

Fortunately, Shirley is not only a romantic lady, but she is a forgiving one, too. We talked about my insensitivity later that night and came to an understanding. I learned a big lesson that Valentine's Day and determined never to forget it. Once I understood how my wife differed from me—especially regarding all things romantic—I began to get with the program.

Your "flame" must be tended with the greatest of care.

It is essential to cultivate a sense of romance if intimacy is to flourish in a marriage. But romance between a husband and wife is precarious. Like the flame of a lone candle burning in the wind, it can easily flicker and die. Your "flame" must be tended with the greatest of care—on Valentine's Day and every other day of the year.

"My Lover Is Mine and I Am His"

The word *romance* conjures up different images for each of us, and our expectations of what constitutes a romantic relationship also vary. Women are inclined to describe romance as the things their mate does to make them feel loved, protected, and respected. Wives, especially those married to busy husbands, crave the excitement of romantic encounters. They long for "some enchanted evening, across a crowded room." Flowers, compliments, nonsexual touching, and love notes are all steps in this direction. So is helping out at home. A man who shares in the duties of cooking, cleaning, and picking up the kids after basketball practice is much more likely to win the affection of his wife.

Men, on the other hand, rely more on their senses in the area of romance. They appreciate a wife who makes herself as attractive to him as possible. A man wants to be respected—and even better, admired—by his wife. He likes to hear his wife express genuine interest in his opinions, hobbies, and work.

Perhaps the most evocative descriptions of romantic love come from Solomon's Song of Songs, where we see that it includes both intimacy and emotional excitement: "My lover is mine and I am his" (2:16) and "My heart began to pound for him" (5:4). We see how deep affection inspires desire and complete appreciation for another:

"How beautiful you are, my darling!" (4:1). We learn that to be romantic means to pursue the object of our affection—and to pine when he or she eludes us: "All night long on my bed I looked for the one my heart loves; I looked for him but did not find him" (3:1). And we see how powerfully a public display of affection communicates romantic love: "He has taken me to the banquet hall, and his banner over me is love" (2:4).

Though romance can mean vastly different things to each of us, for most the word describes that wonderful feeling of being noticed, wanted, and pursued—of being at the very center of our lover's attention. Typically, most couples maintain this sense of romance throughout their courtship and at least through the newlywed phase of marriage. As the years go by and new duties and responsibilities pile on, however, that romantic feeling all too often begins to fade.

The Thrill of the Chase

Whether a few days, weeks, or months after the wedding, something begins to happen to "that lovin' feeling." A man and woman just seem to lose the wind in their romantic sails. It does not always occur, but too often it does.

Their plight reminds me of seamen back in the days of wooden vessels. Sailors in that era had much to fear, including pirates, storms, and diseases. But their greatest fear was that the ship might encounter the Doldrums. The Doldrums was an area of the ocean near the equator characterized by calm and very light shifting winds. It could mean death for the entire crew. The ship's food and water supply would be exhausted as they drifted for days, or even weeks, waiting for a breeze to put them back on course.

Well, marriages that were once exciting and loving can also get caught in the romantic doldrums, causing a slow and painful death to the relationship. But it need not be so. Author Doug Fields, in his book *Creative Romance*, writes, "Dating and romancing your spouse can change those patterns, and it can be a lot of fun. There's no quick fix to a stagnant marriage, of course, but you can lay aside the excuses and begin to date your sweetheart."[7] In fact, you might want to try thinking like a teenager again. Let me explain.

Recall for a moment the craziness of your dating days—the coy attitudes, the flirting, the fantasies, the chasing after the prize. As we moved from courtship to marriage, most of us felt we should grow up and leave the game-playing behind. But we may not have matured as much as we'd like to think.

In some ways, our romantic relationships will always bear some characteristics of adolescent sexuality. Adults still love the thrill of the chase, the lure of the unattainable, excitement of the new and boredom with the old. Immature impulses are controlled and minimized in a committed relationship, of course, but they never fully disappear.

This could help you keep vitality in your marriage. When things have grown stale between you and your spouse, maybe you should remember some old tricks. How about breakfast in bed? A kiss in the rain? Rereading those old love letters together? A night at a bed and breakfast? Roasting marshmallows by an open fire? Cooking a meal together that you've never tried before? A phone call in the middle of the day? A long-stem rose and a love note? There are dozens of ways to fill the sails with wind once more.

I recall one occasion—many years after that unfortunate first Valentine's Day—when Shirley and I explored what we called our "old haunts." We took an entire day together, beginning with a visit to the Farmer's Market, where we had strolled as young lovers. Then we had a leisurely lunch at a favorite restaurant and talked of things long ago. Afterwards we saw a theater performance at the Pasadena Playhouse, where we had gone on our second date, and later we had cherry pie and coffee at Gwinn's restaurant, a favorite hangout for dating couples. We talked about our warm memories and relived the excitement of earlier days. It was a wonderful reprise.

Another time, when I had been away from Shirley and our children for two weeks, I planned a little surprise for her. I asked her to be ready to go to dinner when I flew back home. Then I called Shirley's mother and asked her to be prepared to spend the night with the children, but to make Shirley think they were coming home late.

After we had gone to dinner and the theater that evening, I drove us to a beach community where I had made reservations at a hotel. Shirley didn't catch on until I opened the door and invited her to join me. That evening is still a favorite memory for us. (You see, I really *have* learned a thing or two over the years!)

Enjoy together your own unique brand of romance.

Even when finances are tight, just being together with your partner can rekindle that lovin' feeling. All that is needed is a little effort and creative flair. Talk with your mate; ask him or her what would bring new interest and excitement to your marriage. Then enjoy together your own unique brand of romance.

How to Love a Man

Much has been made in recent decades of a man's responsibility to recognize his wife's need for romance. And rightly so. But what should a woman do for a man that will most clearly communicate love to him? In a word, she can build his confidence.

This vital role is best illustrated by one of my favorite stories told by my friend, E. V. Hill. Dr. Hill is a dynamic black minister and the senior pastor at Mount Zion Missionary Baptist Church in Los Angeles. He lost his precious wife, Jane, to cancer a few years ago. In one of the most moving messages I've ever heard, Dr. Hill spoke about Jane at her funeral and described the ways this "classy lady" made him a better man.

As a struggling young preacher, E. V. had trouble earning a living. That led him to invest the family's scarce resources, over Jane's objections, in the purchase of a service station. She felt her husband lacked the time and expertise to oversee his investment, which proved to be accurate. Eventually, the station went broke and E. V. lost his shirt in the deal.

It was a critical time in the life of this young man. He had failed at something important, and his wife would have been justified in saying, "I told you so." But Jane had an intuitive understanding of her husband's vulnerability. Thus, when E. V. called to tell her that he had lost the station, she said simply, "All right."

E. V. came home that night expecting his wife to be pouting over his foolish investment. Instead, she sat down with him and said, "I've been doing some figuring. I figure that you don't smoke and you don't drink. If you smoked and drank, you would have lost as much as you lost in the service station. So, it's six in one hand and a half-dozen in the other. Let's forget it."

Jane could have shattered her husband's confidence at that delicate juncture. The male ego is surprisingly fragile, especially during times of failure and embarrassment. That's why E. V. needed to hear her say, "I still believe in you," and that is precisely the message she conveyed to him.

Shortly after the fiasco with the service station, E. V. came home one night and found the house dark. When he opened the door, he saw that Jane had prepared a candlelight dinner for two.

"What meaneth thou this?" he said with characteristic humor.

"Well," said Jane, "we're going to eat by candlelight tonight."

E. V. thought that was a great idea and went into the bathroom to wash his hands. He tried unsuccessfully to turn on the light. Then he felt his way into the bedroom and flipped another switch. Darkness prevailed. The young pastor went back to the dining room and asked Jane why the electricity was off. She began to cry.

"You worked so hard, and we're trying," said Jane, "but it's pretty tough. I didn't have quite enough money to pay the light bill. I didn't want you to know about it, so I thought we would just eat by candlelight."

Dr. Hill described his wife's words with intense emotion: "She could have said, 'I've never been in this situation before. I was reared in the home of Dr. Caruthers, and we never had our lights cut off.' She could have broken my spirit; she could have ruined me; she could have demoralized me. But instead she said, 'Somehow or another we'll get these lights on. But let's eat tonight by candlelight.'"

Jane Hill must have been an incredible lady. Of her many gifts and attributes, I am most impressed by her awareness of the role she played in strengthening and supporting her husband. E. V. Hill is a powerful Christian leader today. Who would have believed that he needed his wife to build and preserve his confidence? But that is the way men are made. Most of us are a little shaky inside, especially during early adulthood, and we need love as much as anyone.

The Art of Making Love

When a husband and wife achieve true intimacy, of course, they will naturally desire to share their romantic feelings at the deepest level. By God's design, one of the most pleasurable ways for couples to express their profound love and appreciation is through His gift of sexual intimacy.

Some would say that "having sex" and "making love" are one and the same, but there's an important distinction between the two. The physical act of intercourse can be accomplished by any appropriately matched members of the animal kingdom. But the art of making love, as intended by God, is a much more meaningful and complex experience. It is physical, emotional, and spiritual. In marriage we should settle for nothing less than a sexual relationship that is expressed not only body to body, but also heart to heart and soul to soul. This intimate union, two becoming "one flesh," is both the symbol and fruit of genuine, heartfelt romantic love between a husband and wife.

The epitome of deeply felt romantic love—including sexual intimacy—can only be expressed within the unbreakable bond of marriage. We have already read some of Solomon's depictions of romance. His Song of Songs concludes with this eloquent description of the connection between two married lovers: "Love is as strong as death, its jealousy unyielding as the grave. It burns like a blazing fire, like a mighty flame" (8:6).

The epitome of deeply felt romantic love...

can only be expressed within the

unbreakable bond of marriage.

This fiery, romantic, sexually intimate love is not achieved overnight. It develops between a man and woman through a process called *marital bonding*. Such bonding refers to the emotional covenant that links a man and woman together for life and makes them intensely valuable to one another. It is the specialness that sets those two lovers apart from every other couple on the face of the earth. It is God's gift of intimate companionship.

How does this marital bonding occur? According to the research of Dr. Desmond Morris, bonding is most likely to develop among those who have moved systematically and slowly through twelve steps during their courtship and early marriage. These steps begin with the visual connection, then progress to conversation, then to several stages of nonsexual touching, and finally to the last four stages, which are distinctly sexual and private—and reserved for marriage— culminating in intercourse.[8]

What Morris's research shows is that intimacy must proceed slowly if a male-female relationship is to achieve its full potential. When two people love each other deeply and are committed for life, they have usually developed a great volume of understanding between them that would be considered insignificant to anyone else. They share countless private memories unknown to the rest of the world. This is in large measure where their sense of specialness to one another originates. When sexual intercourse occurs without the stages that should have preceded it, the woman, especially, is likely to feel used and abused.

If you are married and now regret that you progressed too quickly toward physical intimacy, it is not too late to go back to the very beginning and rediscover each other anew. I know of no better way to draw close to the person you love. Touching and talking and holding hands and gazing into one another's eyes and building memories are often the best ways to invigorate a tired sex life and renew intimacy.

In fact, men in particular would be wise to recognize that because of the critical physiological and emotional differences between men and women, a woman's sexual desire is aroused by means of these relational types of activities. Unless a woman feels a certain closeness to her husband—unless she believes he respects her as a person—she may be unable to enjoy a sexual encounter with him. A man can contribute immeasurably to his wife's sexual enjoyment—while enhancing his own—by giving time and attention to her emotional needs. He should make plenty of time for romance outside the bedroom. He should understand that fatigue is a sexual "inhibitor" and help his wife find opportunities for emotional and physical restoration. And he will be richly rewarded by doing all he can to build her self-esteem. The strong connection between self-worth and the ability to respond to sexual stimuli means that anything a man does to reduce his wife's self-esteem will probably be translated into bed-room problems. But respect and affirmation will increase her self-confidence and lead to a more fulfilling sex life.[9] The Lord established the insti-tution of marriage and gave us the gift of physical intimacy as a means of expressing love between husband and wife. As designed by Him, the sexual relationship in marriage is much more than an afterthought or a method to guarantee procrea-tion. When characterized by mutual respect, tenderness, and affection, it is the ultimate demon-stration of profound, romantic love between a man and woman. It is also a glue that holds mar-riages together.

No matter how you define and express romance—through flowers, love notes, an evening in the bedroom, or all of the above—it is a vital ingredient for achieving genuine and lasting intimacy in your marriage. If you are careful to nurture and protect the flame of romance in your relationship, you'll enjoy its warmth for a lifetime.

Renewing Your Romance

- Write down what romance means to you and ask your partner to do the same. Now compare notes. You may be surprised at what your spouse comes up with!

- What are your favorite memories of romance with your mate? How could you recapture those? What new memories would you like to make? Schedule at least two of these for sometime in the next two months.

- How often do you and your partner journey through the twelve steps to intimacy? Set aside a relaxed day, evening, or weekend to do exactly that, and pay special attention to each step as you enjoy your time together.

Epilogue

In this small book we have covered many aspects of intimacy in marriage. I hope that you now have a deeper understanding of the complexity and fragility of a heart-to-heart relationship with your partner. I also pray that you have discovered practical and biblical advice and real help within these pages. Though intimacy is not easily achieved or maintained, I can speak from personal knowledge that building a close relationship with one's "soul mate" is one of the most fulfilling experiences you will find on this earth. I will forever be grateful that the Lord led me to Shirley, and her to me.

In hopes that it will encourage you, I leave you with this portrait of the intimacy that my wife and I have enjoyed during our forty-four-year marriage. It is a letter I wrote at a Marriage Encounter seminar we participated in long ago. That weekend we discovered a secret source of tension that Shirley had not verbalized and I didn't know existed. It had to do with the recent deaths of eight senior members of our small family, six of whom were males. My wife had watched as the survivors struggled to cope with life alone and the awesome implications of sudden widowhood. Because Shirley and I were then in our mid-forties, she was quietly worrying about the possibility of losing me—and wanting to know where we were going from here. My loving wife was also saying to herself, *I know Jim needed me when we were younger and he was struggling to establish himself professionally. But do I still have a prominent place in his heart?*

One simply does not sit down to discuss such delicate matters, voice to voice, in the rush and hubbub of everyday life. They are held inside until (and if) an opportunity to express them is provided. For Shirley and me, that occurred at the

Marriage Encounter program. In the early part of the weekend, we worked through the possibility of my death. Then on the final morning, the issue of my continued love for her was laid to rest.

Shirley was alone in our hotel room, expressing her private concern in a written statement to me. And by divine leadership, I'm sure, I was in another room addressing the same issue, even though we had not discussed it. When we came together and renewed our commitment for the future, whatever it might hold, Shirley and I experienced one of the most emotional moments of our lives. It was a highlight of our twenty-one years together, and neither of us will ever forget it.

Although it will require me to share an intensely personal statement between my wife and me, I would like to conclude with a portion of the letter I wrote to her on that memorable morning. I will skip the more intimate details, quoting only the memories that "bonded" me to my bride.

Who else shares the memory of my youth
during which the foundations of love
were laid? I ask you, who else could
occupy the place that is reserved for the

only woman who was there when I grad-
uated from college and went to the army
and returned as a student at USC and
bought my first decent car (and promptly
wrecked it) and picked out an inexpen-
sive wedding ring with you (and paid for
it with savings bonds) and we prayed and
thanked God for what we had? Then we
said the wedding vows and my dad
prayed, "Lord, You gave us Jimmy and
Shirley as infants to love and cherish and
raise for a season, and tonight, we give
them back to you after our labor of
love—not as two separate individuals, but
as one!" And everyone cried.

Then we left for the honeymoon and
spent all our money and came home to
an apartment full of rice and a bell on the
bed, and we had only just begun. You
taught the second grade and I taught (and
fell in love with) a bunch of sixth-graders
and especially a kid named Norbert, and I
earned a master's degree and passed the
comprehensive exams for a doctorate, and
we bought our first little home and

remodeled it, and I dug up all the grass
and buried it in a ten-foot hole which
later sank and looked like two graves in
the front yard—and while spreading the
dirt to make a new lawn, I accidentally
"planted" eight million ash seeds from our
tree and discovered two weeks later that
we had a forest growing between our
house and the street.

Then alas, you delivered our very own
baby and we loved her half to death and
named her Danae Ann and built a room
on our little bungalow and gradually filled
it with furniture. Then I joined the staff
of Children's Hospital, and I did well
there but still didn't have enough money
to pay our USC tuition and other
expenses so we sold (and ate) a
Volkswagen. Then I earned a PhD and we
cried and thanked God for what we had.
In 1970, we brought home a little boy
and named him James Ryan and loved
him half to death and didn't sleep for six
months. And I labored over a manuscript
titled "Dare to" something or other and

then reeled backward under a flood of favorable responses and a few not-so-favorable responses and received a small royalty check and thought it was a fortune, and I joined the faculty at USC School of Medicine and did well there.

Soon I found myself pacing the halls of Huntington Memorial Hospital as a team of grim-faced neurologists examined your nervous system for evidence of a hypothalamic tumor, and I prayed and begged God to let me complete my life with my best friend, and He finally said, "Yes—for now," and we cried and thanked Him for what we had. And we bought a new house and promptly tore it to shreds and went skiing in Vail, Colorado, and tore your leg to shreds, and I called your mom to report the accident and she tore me to shreds, and our toddler, Ryan, tore the whole town of Arcadia to shreds. And the construction on the house seemed to go on forever and you stood in the shattered living room and cried every Saturday night because so little had been accomplished. Then during the worst of the mess, 100 friends gave us a surprise housewarming and they slopped through the debris and mud and sawdust and cereal bowls and sandwich parts—and the next morning you groaned and asked, "Did it really happen?"

And I published a new book called *Hide or Seek* and everyone called it *Hide and Seek* and the publisher sent us to Hawaii and we stood on the balcony overlooking the bay and thanked God for what we had. And I published *What Wives Wish* and people liked it and the honors rolled in and the speaking requests arrived by the hundreds.

Then you underwent risky surgery and I said, "Lord, not now!" And the doctor said, "No cancer!" and we cried and thanked God for what we had. Then I started a radio program and took a leave of absence from Children's Hospital and opened a little office in Arcadia called Focus on the Family, which a three-year-old radio listener later called "Poke us in the Family," and we got more visible.

Then we went to Kansas City for a family vacation and my dad prayed on the last day and said, "Lord, we know it can't always be the wonderful way it is now, but we thank You for the love we enjoy today." A month later he experienced his heart attack and in December I said good-bye to my gentle friend, and you put your arm around me and said, "I'm hurting with you!" and I cried and said "I love you!" And we invited my mother to spend six weeks with us during her recuperation period and the three of us endured the loneliest Christmas of our lives as the empty chair and missing place setting reminded us of his red sweater and domi-noes and apples and a stack of sophisticated books and a little dog named Benji who always sat on his lap. But life went on. My mother staggered to get her-self back together and couldn't and lost fifteen pounds and moved to California and still ached for her missing friend.

And more books were written and more honors arrived and we became better known and our influence spread and we thanked God for what we had. And our daughter went into adolescence and this great authority on children knew he was inadequate and found himself asking God to help him with the awesome task of parenting and He did and we thanked Him for sharing His wisdom with us.

And then a little dog named Siggie who was sort of a dachshund grew old and toothless and we had to let the vet do his thing, and a fifteen-year love affair between man and dog ended with a whimper. But a pup named Mindy showed up at the front door and life went on. Then a series of films were produced in San Antonio, Texas, and our world turned upside down as we were thrust into the fishbowl and "Poke us in the Family" expanded in new directions and life got busier and more hectic and time became more precious, and then someone invited us to a Marriage Encounter weekend where I sit at this moment.

So I ask you! Who's gonna take your place in my life? You have become me and I have become you. We are inseparable. I've now spent 46 percent of my life with you, and I can't even remember much of the first 54! Not one of the experiences I've listed can be comprehended by anyone but the woman who lived through them with me. Those days are gone, but their aroma lingers on in our minds. And with every event during these twenty-one years, our lives have become more intertwined— blending eventually into this incredible affection that I bear for you today.

Is it any wonder that I can read your face like a book when we are in a crowd? The slightest narrowing of your eyes speaks volumes to me about the thoughts that are running through your conscious experience. As you open Christmas presents, I know instantly if you like the color or style of the gift, because your feelings cannot be hidden from me.

I love you, S.M.D. (Remember the

monogrammed shirt?) I love the girl who
believed in me before I believed in myself.
I love the girl who never complained
about huge school bills and books and
hot apartments and rented junky furniture and no vacations and humble little
Volkswagens. You have been *with* me—
encouraging me, loving me, and
supporting me since August 27, 1960.
And the status you have given me in our
home is beyond what I have deserved.

So why do I want to go on living? It's
because I have you to take that journey
with. Otherwise, why make the trip? The
half life that lies ahead promises to be
tougher than the years behind us. It is in
the nature of things that my mom will
someday join my father and then she will
be laid to rest beside him in Olathe,
Kansas, overlooking a windswept hill
from whence he walked with Benji and
recorded a cassette tape for me describing
the beauty of that spot. Then we'll have
to say good-bye to your mom and dad.
Gone will be the table games we played

and the Ping-Pong and lawn darts and
Joe's laughter and Alma's wonderful ham
dinners and her underlined birthday cards
and the little yellow house in Long Beach.
Everything within me screams "No!" But
my Dad's final prayer is still valid: "We
know it can't always be the way it is now."
When that time comes, our childhoods
will then be severed—cut off by the pass-
ing of the beloved parents who bore us.

What then, my sweet wife? To whom
will I turn for solace and comfort? To
whom can I say, "I'm hurting!" and know
that I am understood in more than an
abstract manner? To whom can I turn
when the summer leaves begin to change
colors and fall to the ground? How much
I have enjoyed the springtime and the
warmth of the summer sun. The flowers
and the green grass and the blue sky and
the clear streams have been savored to
their fullest. But alas, autumn is coming.
Even now, I can feel a little nip in the
air—and I try not to look at a distant,
lone cloud that passes near the horizon.

I must face the fact that winter lies ahead, with its ice and sleet and snow to pierce us through. But in this instance, winter will not be followed by springtime, except in the glory of the life to come. With whom, then, will I spend that final season of my life?

None but you, Shirls. The only joy of the future will be in experiencing it as we have the past twenty-one years—hand in hand with the one I love…a young miss named Shirley Deere, who gave me everything she had—including her heart.

Thank you, babe, for making this journey with me. Let's finish it—together!

Your Jim

5 Essentials for Lifelong Intimacy

1. Establishing a Christ-Centered Home

2. Cultivating Committed Love

3. Building Trust Together

4. Seeking to Understand

5. Renewing Your Romance

Notes

1. Divorce, Provisional 1998 data, National Center for Health Statistics. http://www.cdc.gov/nchs/fastats/divorce.html (accessed January 13, 2003).

2. Robertson McQuilkin, *A Promise Kept* (Wheaton, IL: Tyndale House Publishers, 1998), 19–23.

3. M. O. Vincent, "The Physician's Own Well-Being," *Annals Royal College of Physicians and Surgeons of Canada 1981*, vol. 14, 4, 277–281.

4. James Dobson, *What Wives Wish Their Husbands Knew About Women* (Wheaton, IL: Tyndale House Publishers, 1975), 78.

5. Gary Smalley and John Trent, *The Language of Love* (Pomona, CA: Focus on the Family Publishing, 1988).

6. Chuck and Barb Snyder, *Incompatibility: Still Grounds for a Great Marriage* (Sisters, OR: Multnomah Publishers, 1999).

7. Doug Fields, *Creative Romance* (Eugene, OR: Harvest House Publishers, 1991), 15, as stated in James Dobson, *Solid Answers* (Wheaton, IL: Tyndale House Publishers, 1997), 557.

8. Desmond Morris, *Intimate Behavior* (New York: Random House, 1971).

9. Dobson, *What Wives Wish Their Husbands Knew About Women*, paraphrased from 116, 124–129.

7 SOLUTIONS FOR BURNED-OUT PARENTS

Dr. James Dobson offers practical advice for burned-out parents. Parents will be renewed as they find more time to enjoy life, nurture their families, and develop a more meaningful relationship with the Lord.

www.mpbooks.com

BUILD A MARRIAGE THAT WILL GO THE DISTANCE

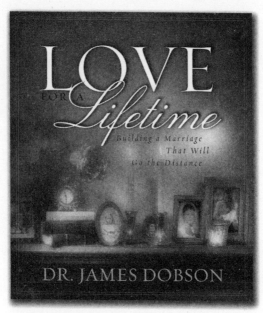

1-59052-087-4

This bestselling classic has brought hope, harmony, and healing to millions of homes for more than fifteen years. Strengthen and celebrate your own marriage with Dr. James Dobson's powerful insights!